LYNI

Man Code

The code of conduct between men

Also known as
"guy code," "man law" and "dude rules"

Man Code: The code of conduct between men
Also known as "guy code," "man law" and "dude rules" by Lynn Sanderson

Published by Lynn Sanderson

First Edition April 2022

Book Layout and Cover Design
by Suzanne Fyhrie Parrott

Cover Graphics:
Flourish by @ Provectors, Depositphotos.com
Black Man Logo Design @ G234TD4Y,
Shutterstock.com

ISBN: 978-0-578-38172-5 (pbk)

*Printed in the
United States of America*

From the Author:

This book is a compilation of man code rules for the dedicated, loyal and resourceful men who live by the words of wisdom on the following pages.

This book is dedicated to
Wayne Woodard, one of the true
Keepers of the Code.

First rule about

man code:

Don't talk about man code.

A man should just "know"

man code by extension of

being a man.

There should never be any written evidence of a man code, nor any conversation pertaining to its existence.

If the topic of man code should arise in any conversation where even one person present is not a man, the topic should be avoided completely or even denied.

Even if there *was* evidence

(either spoken or written)

alluding to the

existence of man code,

it should never come

from a woman.

A man's

gotta have a code.

Real men follow man code

100% of the time.

If you only follow man code

when it suits you, then

you are not a real man.

It is equally possible to both respect another man's code and mock the discrepancies between your code and his.

You must never torpedo single friends.

Death before dishonor.

Don't bring a knife

to a gun fight.

If you can fix it

before anyone notices

the damage,

then nothing happened.

Make your own options.

Know your fight level.

Examples:

Nothing below the belt.

Not the face!

Kidneys are wild.

Anything goes.

Do what needs to be done

to accomplish the mission.

A handshake between *real men* is as good as a legally binding contract.

If you break the deal,

be prepared for whatever

consequences occur

as a result.

There are two paths in life:

One is winning or learning.

The other is losing.

If you can't swim,

don't fall out of the boat.

If your wife or girlfriend

likes Píña Coládas

and getting caught in

the rain, *then you like*

those things too.

If she doesn't say

"do it now" then

technically it can be

done *whenever*.

Whoever's wife

(or girlfriend) calls

or texts first on poker

night gets to buy

everyone a round.

If you see another

man's zipper down,

don't say anything.

That's his problem.

Never go back

on your word.

All a man has is his word.

Discretion is

the better part of valor.

Always pump fake it.

It might buy you

a first down.

A man's gotta know

another man's

limitations.

Screw your courage

to the sticking place.

If there are two women in the car giving you directions, and neither can agree, you have two choices:

Follow directions from the one you're going home with, or pretend to be deaf.

Adopt the phrase:

“Let me show you how we do things where I come from.”

Real men never

use nursery words in

conversation with other men

(such as “tummy,” “icky” or “poopy.”)

If you owe someone a favor,

you must honor that favor

upon request.

Any time, any place,

anywhere.

If you break

man code rules,

you have to turn in

your man card.

It's okay if a girl wants

to touch your car/ride/

tractor/motorcycle/etc.

Another man better keep

his hands to himself.

If it doesn’t fit,

get a bigger hammer.

There is one important decision that must be made before every battle:

If loss is imminent, will you choose to die on that hill, or live to fight another day?

A real man would

rather die covered in

blood on the battlefield,

than as an old man

lying in his own piss.

When it's all over,

pick up your brass.

Remember to give the getaway driver a cut of the spoils.

If you don't have the opportunity to make hostile intentions known, then a warning shot is a perfectly acceptable way to convey those intentions.

Sometimes you just

gotta take a punch.

Getting crushed by

a compactor hurts less

than a broken heart.

Take care of your shit.*

* “Shit” being defined as anything you are responsible for: your car, your laundry, or the birthday present that you stupidly agreed to find for your mother-in-law's birthday.

Don’t mess

with another man’s shit.

Always have

Plan B.

If it's not a fair fight,

you don't get any credit

for winning.

Men do what they must

and call it by the

best of names.

If you want peace,

prepare for war.

As long as no one dies or is seriously injured, it's okay to laugh at another man's pain.

Throw another pallet

on the fire.

Have the decency

not to fuck up.

Depending on

what generation you

are from . . .

Load and lock.

Or lock and load.

If the situation warrants it, have the courage and decency to fall on your sword.

Kicking another man

in the balls is a dick move.

Have the decency

to condemn a man to his face;

do not go behind his back.

If you are double-dog dared to do something, you are contractually obligated to go through with it.

If you meet a foe in battle and you both survive until sundown, man code dictates that you can now share a friendly drink together.

Until the sun rises

the next day.

Never shoot prey

while it's sleeping.

It's unsportsmanlike.

Nobody wants

to take point.

But *everyone* has to take a turn.

If you want to be successful,

sometimes you gotta

be an asshole.

(Nice guys finish last.)

When asked to perform a toast at your best friend's wedding, the toast should be tailored to the bride's standards, not the groom's.

If you are questioned by a friend's wife or girlfriend regarding your friend's whereabouts, you should never reveal any details.

You are also allowed to deny that you even know him.

Make good on your promises, especially if they correlate to any of the man code laws.

Two men may never

share an umbrella

or a drink.

Never borrow another

man's underwear.

Men can never go to the

restroom together.

Unless it's halftime,

and then it's a race.

Body paint on a large stomach is perfectly acceptable.

Body paint on a shirtless torso can also be considered proper man attire, which can overturn the “no shirt, no service” rule.

Sometimes you

gotta man up.

Men can never apply

suntan lotion on other men.

Women, on the other hand, are

allowed to put suntan lotion

on each other because it's cute.

Don't blow another

man's cover.

Unless he's a dick and

deserves it.

You poke it,

you own it.

Under no circumstances*

are you ever allowed to date

your best friend's

ex-girlfriend.

*This rule is frequently challenged based on extenuating circumstances that are considered on a case-by-case basis.

Some exceptions include: your best friend dated his ex for less than 24 hours; you didn't come on to the ex, she came on to *you*; the ex-girlfriend is super hot and happens to love beer and football.

Under no circumstances* are you ever allowed to date your best friend's sister.

*This rule can **never** be challenged. If challenged, the challenger will have no choice but to marry his best friend's sister.

Unless under extreme crisis conditions, always keep your emotions in check.

Moodiness is for chicks.

If chosen to be someone's

wing man, you must accept all

of the consequences

of that title, including,

but not limited to:

Sleeping with the ugly

girlfriend of your friend's

intended target.

Your friend may never speak of your misfortunes of the incident, should any misfortunes occur.*

*except when sharing humorous stories of conquest among an all-male group of good friends.

If your buddy is running late,

you are under no obligation

to wait for him.

If your girlfriend or wife

is running late, she can be

as late as she wants.

Remembering birthdays and/or giving gifts to your friends is optional.

No matter how bad the movie, no man must ever speak ill of films starring manly dudes playing manly roles.

(Think Burt Reynolds, Bruce Lee, John Wayne, Samuel Jackson, Sylvester Stallone, Chuck Norris and Jackie Chan, just to name a few.)

When visiting your buddy's place, feel free to help yourself to the fridge. But *never* take the last beer.

If the wind should blow

a skirt up, and you

happen to notice, then

you are merely an

innocent benefactor of a

chance circumstance.

If two (or more) men

wish to fight,

do not interfere.

But feel free

to place wagers.

Whether in an argument or a fight, do not come to your buddy's defense unless invited to do so.

If your buddy is arguing

with his wife or girlfriend,

you are forbidden

to back him up.

He's on his own.

The answer to every

wife or girlfriend's question

regarding their apparel

(ie: "Does this dress make

me look fat?") is:

"Dear, you look amazing."

Special thanks for inspiration to:

Bruce Wayne, Dan "The Man",
Chuck Norris, The A-Team,
Clint Eastwood, John Wayne,
Bruce Lee, Indiana Jones,
Arnold Schwarzenegger,
Steve McQueen, Al Pacino,
Robert Mitchum, the dudes of
M*A*S*H, Humphrey Bogart,
Daniel Boone, James Bond,
Sylvester Stallone, Wesley Snipes,

Robert De Niro, James Cagney,
Samuel L. Jackson, Vegeta,
Dwayne Johnson,
Bruce Willis, Charlton Heston,
Lee Marvin, Tommy Lee Jones,
Danny Trejo, Charles Bronson,
Antonio Banderas, Skipper,
Teddy Roosevelt, Hugh Jackman,
Kurt Russell, Sean Connery,
Mel Gibson, Russel Crowe,
Alex Louis Armstrong,
Vin Diesel, Sean Penn,
the Marlboro Man and so many
more names worth mentioning,
but there's just too many to count.

With additional credits to:

MTV's series Guy Code

Miller Lite's Men of the Square Table commercials

Urban Dictionary's Guy Code

Made in the USA
Columbia, SC
07 October 2024